POET COET

A Poetry and Short Story Collection

Ed Coet

Published by
The Blue Fog Journal
Lulu Press Inc

Published by *The Blue Fog Journal*
in association with *Lulu Press*

First Edition

Book layout and design: Rohitash Chandra
Cover design: Ed Coet and Rohitash Chandra

Copies are also available for purchase via the internet in major online stores.

The Blue Fog Journal
editor@bluefogjournal.com
www.bluefogjournal.com

Library of Congress Control Number: 2008908107

ISBN: 978-0-6152-4211-8

Forward

The poetry and short-stories of Ed Coet have appeared in magazines and journals around the world. This first ever compilation of his work was long overdue and much awaited. Ed Coet has emerged as a respected international poet and freelance writer of enviable reputation. His style is unique and diverse. His poems take the reader on a roller coaster of emotions that inspire and motivate one to laugh, cry, cheer or dwell in deep contemplative, philosophical and introspective thought. His short stories captivate youths and are a fun read for adults. This *Poet Coet* collection is a remarkable work of talent. It will make an impression in the repository of fine literature. Without doubt, Ed's poetry and short-story fans will indulge in this literary treat. Finally, Ed Coet shows a deep commitment to poetry through his contribution as the editor of the Blue Fog Journal. Blue Fog Journal readers and writers are indebted to his efforts.

Sincerely,

Rohitash Chandra,

Founding Editor, Blue Fog Journal

Author, "A Hot Pot of Roasted Poems"

Acknowledgements

I wish to acknowledge my mother, Ernestine H. Coet, and my brother, Walter P. Coet - my greatest fans and supporters. I also wish to thank my dear friend Daniel Graham, a consummate novelist, for his advice and assistance over the years. I am especially grateful to Blue Fog Journal founding editor, Rohitash Chandra, for his editing, layout and book design assistance. I thank the Blue Fog Journal for making this publication a reality. Most of all I wish to thank all *Poet Coet* fans for their support and encouragement. With appreciation to all, I am -

ED COET
The Poet Coet

Dedication

For my wife, Eve,
and our daughters Tara and Paula.

Contents

Part I: Poetry

Part I: Poetry continued

Part II: Short Stories

Poet Coet Biographical Sketch

Part I
Poetry

Perfect Love

It cannot be diminished,
regulated or rationed.
It is eternal.
It doesn't develop,
it is born within.
It is unconditional.
It trusts.
It is never jealous
and it doesn't brag;
It is kind, polite,
pure, humble,
and always right.
It embraces truth
and rejects evil.
It is powerful,
patient, honest
and forgiving.
Perfect love
is forever perfect.

Moment

The moment I saw you,
the instinct I captured that first
glimpse of breathtaking beauty it
shook me to the depth of my soul,
to the core of my being,
and I thought I would explode in ecstasy.

The moment I caught a glimpse
of your glimmering smile,
and felt the penetrating warmth
of your essence, purity and goodness,
your kindness and charm,
I was captivated body and soul.

That was the moment I was drawn in.
I was over come by an imaginary truth
that I could not explain and
could only feel and experience.
It explained that one emotion
that everyone seeks. It explained love.

That moment could not be denied me.
It could never be diminished or dismissed.
It was wholly mine to cling to
for however long I wanted.
It was complete perfection.
It was the moment I dreamt you.

Wife

I awoke to your beauty
after sleeping with my desire
and I knew in an instant,
at that precious moment
that you were the dream
that would fulfill my life
with love and passion
because you agreed
to become my wife.

Touch

May I touch you?
Can I clasp you hand and kiss you fingers?
May I stoke your hair and bring you close?
Will you allow me to embrace you?
May I touch you?

Can you feel me?
Can you feel my heartbeat, my rapid pulse?
The sensual joy I extend to you?
The rapturous warmth of my whole being?
Can you feel me?

Do you know me?
Do you understand who I am, my essence?
How much I desire, want, and need you;
the spiritual depth of my love for you?
Do you know me?

May I touch you?
Can I reach for you and bring you close?
Will you allow my gentle embrace?
My titillating caress? A tender kiss of passion?
May I touch you?

Daughters

A providential miracle,
she captivated me
from birth.
She embodied
innocence and
wholesome purity
of such sublime quality
that I instantly knew
only God could create
such an extraordinary wonder.

I felt like a child
with his first pet
when I saw her
and I was drawn to her
like a magnet of love
that bonded and sealed
human life.

I was compelled to
cuddle this creative
miracle and marvel at
God's handicraft.
From that moment on
she would forever be
the special entity
I called "precious pet."

When her sister arrived
I was beside myself
with pride.
Immersed in gratitude
and drenched in joy
I could hardly fathom
my good fortune.

Sweet as sugar
and cuddly like a bear,
she possessed a sparkle and
spirit that defined fun
and spelled felicity.
From that very instant
she would forever be
my precious –
little "Sugar-bear."

Like a trophy case
with twin Oscars
these sibling darlings
would grow in to my
proudest accomplishment.
They were and remain
inestimable female prizes
that would make any dad
beam with pride
and proudly proclaim -
"that's my daughter!"

Grandma

I know the joy of a sunny day
        when kids go out for fun and play,
        the joy of being happy and gay;
        I know cause you're my grandma.

I know how to give a pleasant smile,
        how to twinkle my eyes and tilt a brow.
        To blush with shyness all the while;
        I know cause you're my grandma.

I know the importance of learning in school,
        and doing my chores and being cool.
        Acting good instead of a fool;
        I know cause you're my grandma.

My mom taught me these and other things;
        she even taught me how to sing.
        But first she learned from you I think;
        I know cause you're my grandma.

So I owe you grandma, for my joy in life,
        for raising my mom who gave me life.
        Without you I could never be;
        I know cause you're my grandma.

Golden

They walked together
hand-in-hand
down a golden path
through trials and tribulations,
through hopes and dreams,
joy and fear;
with mutual sacrifice
and collective determination.
With passion, purpose
and enduring love
they remained united
for half a century
in a beautiful relationship
that made them one.

Silver

Blanketed in silver
and engulfed in love,
for a quarter century
they molded a family
and built a life
together as one
in blessed matrimony
that cherished love,
offered hope,
emanated joy,
and defined the purpose
and meaning of marriage.

Penetration

Penetration
In to your eyes, your mind
In to your body, your soul.

Touching
Your thoughts, your feelings
Your skin, your sensitivities.

Feeling
Your heartbeat, your pulse
Your warmth, your love.

We are
One, in love
Together, forever.

Touch of Love

Enigmatic to the senses,
eliciting a titillating response.
Erotically arousing
yet passionately reticent.
Romantically sensual
with deep rapturous warmth.
Shivering with joy felt
to the core of your being,
to the point of weeping.
Spiritual in depth, nearing adoration;
so magnificent is the "touch of love."

Comfort

When I first met you I couldn't leave you,
not even in my thoughts.
Nothing has changed. You are still there.

Without you I was nothing.
With you, everything.
You made me.

If I wakened in the night, regardless of reason,
I reached for you. Like a child in need of nurturing,
the sight of you gave me comfort.

I recall combat in the sands of Desert Storm.
There you were, in my heart and mind.
Still, you gave me comfort.

I see you in our children.
How they look and act. How they live their lives.
They are one with you as you are one with me.

We grew old together.
That was a blessing. Life was wonderful,
but only because I had you.

In the hospital when I was gravelly ill -
there you were, by my bedside.
You were the cure that I needed.

God made me say good-bye.
It hurts. I still cry.
Yet, even in death you give me comfort.

Pride

Pride - oh enemy of humility
be gone ye foundation sin.
Leave me oh dreaded friend
of the dark angel Lucifer.
I will conquer you, oh evil pride.

Away with you, be gone
oh mighty transgression
which seeks always to be extolled,
with honor and praise -
and preference above all
ye undeserving braggart,
oh monstrous boaster
from the depths of hell,
you cling with greed for
glory and unworthy adoration.

Be gone I say
oh selfish beast,
with your shameful
lust for love and pity,
approval and desire.
Oh how ye cowardly flee
rebuke and humiliation.
Always fearful to
be forgotten or
worse - despised.

Wholly worthy of your
calumniation are ye
oh friend of evil, of
the egotistical and
self-indulgent narcissist.
Ye are the enemy of good
and the antithesis of the
worthy and the humble.
Leave me in humility
ye wretched pride.

Hope

A feeling of what can be,
what will turn out for the best,
where expectations are centered
and where forgiveness lives.
A desire that dwells in confidence
with trust as its expectation.
Where spirituality resides
with faith at its core.
It is real, surreal,
moving and magnificent.
It is a special blessing
this feeling of hope.

Restoration

It is a mystery
yet it is real,
confused with the desire
to be made new
or to camouflage the old.
It is satisfied
with what began,
with preference for
the original plan.
It only desires
to be made whole,
to restore energy,
hope, and soul.
It is phenomenal
this restoration goal.

Soldier

I saw a burial with a bugler playing taps;
I turned to my father, "What happened?" I asked.
He clutched my hand and with a quiver in his voice,
he began to explain and his eyes became moist.

"My son," he said, "This is rather difficult for me;
for an old veteran like myself this is tough to see.
In that coffin lies a genuine patriotic warrior,
an honest-to-God hero, an American soldier.

I appreciate that soldier and the service he gave,
and I honor his sacrifice as he's laid in his grave.
He was honorable, selfless, courageous, and bold;
please remember him son, as you grow old.

The value of his service, I must explain,
if not remembered, will be lost in vain.
As a nation we're nothing without soldiers like him;
and failing to remember would be a terrible sin."

I listened in awe as my father spoke,
it seemed as if his heart were broke.
I suddenly remembered when he went to war
and when he returned I thought nothing more.

I never asked why he walked with a limp
and I didn't care about why he was sick.
I was too busy enjoying the life that I had
to realize that I had it because of dad.

I finally understood what my dad was about
and it hurt so bad I cried out loud.
He sacrificed so much so I could be free
and his battle scars were suffered for me.

It was my father's spirit that spoke to me that day;
thank God I finally understood what he had to say.
I saluted his coffin as they laid him to rest
and I thought about the medals pinned on his chest.

That I didn't honor him sooner I will always regret,
and I pledged that day to never again forget.
I'm proud that my dad was a patriotic warrior;
I'm honored to be the son of an American soldier.

Old Glory

Flying high and
waving proudly;
perched atop
a silver orifice
the magnificent
and beautiful
flag of honor -
Old Glory,
smiles upon
a grateful nation
with resplendent
dignity and distinction.

Distant Warrior

I get this wondrous chill as night falls
in mountains or desert sand
and I find myself dreaming about
home, my fondest memory
from this far away land.

I miss the special lady who
stole my heart, my thoughts
and all there is of me;
and I deeply cherish
our final moments together.

I think about the children
I left behind, how I miss them
and pray they're fine -
and it's hard Lord,
it's so very hard.

It's times like this that I wonder
why I volunteered and I
get this knot in my stomach -
then I cringe and find myself
trying to hold back tears.

Soon the battle will begin
when I'll hear my own heartbeat
through the creepy sounds
amidst treacherous mountain sides or
drifting sands and whirling winds.

It's time spent in worry,
fear, and some regret
as I encounter my fate
in the war so near
and I must admit, I'm scared.

This stench of war,
the sight of it all,
it's that awful image
of how I imagined hell
after Lucifer's fall.

I wonder to myself,
"Does it have to be
that generations of people
can't seem to agree
to the simple concept of peace?"

Soldiers don't start wars
but they surely fight them,
making all manner of sacrifice
and I doubt that even once
did a soldier ever like them."

Then I think of "Old Glory"
and I'm filled with pride.
It's a warm patriotic feeling
which overcomes me
from deep down inside.

I'm confused, scared
and battle weary.
I worry about those I love
as I cling to my faith
and pray to God above.

I'm a distant warrior,
an American fighting man;
not an aspiring hero,
but just a simple soldier
trying to do the best that I can.

Happiness

What do you wish for?
Do you wish for that which
you think will make you happy?
Do you reminisce about happier times?
Yesterday is just a memory of what was,
not what is. If happiness is there then it's dead.

Do you wish for a brighter future?
Does happiness live there?
Can you hope happiness in to being?
Do you know what makes you happy?
If not, you're destined to be without it.
You can't experience what you don't know.
You can't discover happiness "out there."

Happiness is an internal adventure.
You can't experience "it" if you
don't know what "it" is.
Laughter is a consequence of happiness
but not happiness itself.
Happiness is a state of mind
not a commodity that can
be bought or sold.
Nobody can make you laugh
if you reject humor or
your soul is devoid of joy.

Happy people experience joy
even if indigent or in hardship.
The wealthy are sometimes miserable
even when dwelling in the lap of luxury.
Joy is the essence of happiness
that is expressed by pleasing others.

Happiness is spiritual – it engulfs you.
It is a journey, not a destination.
Enjoy this splendid and wonderful venture.
Today was yesterday's future and
tomorrow may not arrive.
The time to be happy is now.

Poetry

An instrument of beauty,
poetry is art at its best
with its verses of passion
penned with love
in assorted and variegated
metrical composition
with sublime and
aesthetically satisfying flow.

It is a creative exposition
that unfolds and enlightens
with enchanting constructs
the demonstrative and
effusive characterization
of language by utilizing,
promoting and bestowing
the nature and power of words.

Proclaiming ideas and ideals
of principled excellence
with creations anew
and history of old,
poetry exhibits an appetite
for knowledge and wisdom
and a profound propensity
for purposeful revelation
with an insatiable desire
for intimation and meaning
displayed with heartfelt emotion.

With its aspiration to show case
in magnificent scribal splendor,
poetry entices and compels
the artist and consumer
to explore and transcend
imagination and intrigue,
and solicit introspection
with unfathomable penetrating thought
that is calmed by grace and elegance.

Philosophical and spiritual,
entertaining and healing,
poetry commands laughter and tears
or sorrow and joy.
It's clamorous and powerful
phonologically expressive morphemes
can awaken and stir passion and romance
or summon logic and reason.

Poetry,
resplendent in wisdom,
captures love,
inspires hope,
provokes curiosity,
resonates drama,
evokes mystery,
uplifts spirits
and expresses grief.

So magnificent,
so powerful,
so wondrous
is the nature and
the majesty of poetry.

Keltoi– Celtic Warrior

Charge! He yelled in Goideli as he led in tribal tribal kilt.
The Celtic warrior advanced with determined fighting spirit.
Boldly challenging his fears, facing the valiant Saxon struggle,
he prepared for resistance.

He compelled his coercive compulsion
to fight for honor and to become valid.
Mortally wounded in fierce fighting
he accepted his fate, his eminent death.

From the depth of his pain and suffering
he summed his strength and courage.
With one final breath he screamed in Gaelic,
"God bless the Irish."

dea dhuit, clanadad eireinnan!

Mental Forest

I tapped my mind
and inside
lived a mental forest.

I couldn't see through the
dense forest of trees
and leaves trickling down.

I listened in awe
as I heard
those leaves
falling down
like tiny nuggets
hitting the ground
where their seeds
were swept amongst
the trees in a
fascinating mental breeze.

As they caressed and
hugged the ground
I finally understood
what I had learned
from these seeds
of knowledge
stored safely
in the trunk of memory.

Addict

Petty and ephemeral is the addict
lost in inner space and
devoid of rationality.
A cognitive aberration with listless core;
A captive to lifeless substance.

A begging petitioner of undeserved pity;
wholly blameful for a schism with
all who matter.
A renegade from normality; woefully
ignominious - a trite revulsion.

A perpetual thief to even kin is this
slug of slight substance.
A ruinous parasite to all, including self.
Such is the essence, the very soul of the addict
unless he rejuvenate and change.

Leaders

Trailblazers and bellwethers
who conduct with dignity
are these noble maestros
who shepard people.
Honorable and selfless
luminaries are these bold
inspirers of confidence.
Captains of courage
who lead by example.
Directors who orchestrate,
motivate, excite and
spark others to follow.
Emanate role models
of noteworthy distinction.
These are leaders,
champions of the best
who are as rare
as they are great.

Courage

Summon the strength
to confront pain, grief;
to endure danger
or the threat thereof.
Campaign with determination
to face a valiant struggle.
Boldly challenge the fear within
to prepare for resistance
with instinctive
physiological response.
Compel a coercive compulsion
to become valid.
Assume risk when others retreat.
Stand for righteousness
in the face of adversity.
This is the nature of courage.

Anger

A poignant sense of regret
keenly felt to the core of ones being.
Eliciting archaic emotions,
evoking a corrupt heart.

Summoning the latent potential
of all that is evil within.
Tempting rage
with a vehement desire to lash out.

Feelings of hostility
with displeasing vexation.
Delicate, even fragile sensitivities
accompanied by shattered sensibilities.

An inability to appreciate and
unable to respond to aesthetic influences.
Grudging spite
with offending annoyance.

An intensive force
influencing restricted control;
giving cause for regret
- for guilt filled remorse.

Oh yes,
I know anger.

Stressed

The despair brought about
by mental confusion
more then upsets,
it is emotionally disruptive.
It is like fighting for control of
your mental faculties
as you attempt to target
the source of your anguish
before it take its final toll.

Your heart pounds;
it races like a speeding
locomotive without breaks.
Your blood pressure
explodes like an internal
volcanic eruption.
Your muscles tighten as
if wrapped in a straight jacket
or encased in a soaked glove.

You feel irritable, perplexed
and increasingly depressed
as anxiety challenges for
control of your mind.
You grasp your head
in fearful confusion;
you grow distraught
and desperate for relief.

You deplore this distress,
this foreboding and
solicitous anxiousness
that robs you of your
contentment and comfort.
You can't control the vexation,
the perplexing awful angst
that makes you stressed.

Migraine

Imagine your head
being crunched in a vice.
Visualize the agonizing pounding
as it rips through your brain
like a sledge hammer
trying to fracture your skull
from the inside out.
Can you see your mind fog
as the aura's numb?
Do they paralyze
the side of you face?
Can you feel your eyes strain?
Does the horrific pain
scream out – Stop!
Dear God
make it stop!
If so, you understand
the nature of a migraine.

Boredom

When time is stagnate and the world is on hold.
When feelings of anxiousness emanate from the
search for something in the midst of nothing.
When one grasps for anything to stimulate their
conscious and unconscious thoughts; attempting to
find meaning in a mental void,
a hollow and valueless space in time.
When one clings to a futile effort to make sense
out of a confusing fog of emptiness only to be
ravaged by hollow thoughts. Then and only then
have they experienced true boredom.

Knowledge

To conquer doubt and find reason in the absurd.
To rationalize confusion; make sense out of the illogical.
To define, explain, and understand the misunderstood.
To solve life's mysteries; resolve unanswered questions.
To transcend space; breach the conscious and unconscious.
To understand anything and to know everything.
To acquire complete knowledge.
Simply answer how and why?

Soul

I am wandering, lost in a
forest of confused thoughts;
searching and hoping to discover
the composition of who I am.

I am curious about what
I will find, what it will mean,
and I'm little frightened about
discovering that hidden part of me.

I can see my image but
my soul is hidden. I wonder,
is soul a part of self?
Are they one and the same?

I wonder, do ghosts dwell
within these temples we
call our bodies? Are they
also a reflection of self?

Does this explain our spirit?
If so, are we responsible for it?
Can "it" sin if "it" is a
part of our inner self?

I need enlightenment to
understand this dimension
of the great spiritual mystery
that connects us to our soul.

Morton

Their once was a guy named Morton
who lived in a town called Thornton.
He thought he didn't need
to learn how to read.
He wouldn't do his math
and he always skipped class.
He dropped out of school
and became the town fool.
He didn't know what to do,
because he didn't have a clue
on how to make ends meet
because he couldn't compete
knowing nothing at all
except how to crawl
on bended knee
crying "help me please!'
I ruined my life,
I don't have a wife,
no home to share,
this burden I bare
I'm just a rover
who wants to start over."
But it was too late -
Morton met his fate.
He was still so young
but Morton's life was done.
Poor poor Morton
didn't know what was important.

Sopher Woffer

A tiny little friend of mine
is a Yorkie-Shi Zu canine.
Sopher Woffer I named this dog
even though I know it's odd.
She's very cute and so petite,
my Sopher Woffer's just a treat.
The unconditional love she gives
is a blessing to the life I live.
I never thought this dog could be
so special and important to me.
This Yorkie-Shi Zu canine blend
explains why dogs are mans best friend.
Priceless is the joy I get
from my tiny Sopher Woffer pet.

Orange Cat

Just an ol' Tom Cat
dirty orange in color,
Rummaging like a rat
through filth and squalor

Painfully moving with an obvious limp
and a single eye from which to glimpse.
Orange cat advanced with a hesitant skimp;
so sorrowful a cat I haven't seen since.

Confused and frightened
I could sense his pain.
Sorrowful and disheartened
he began to fain.

Without value or worth,
abandoned and alone,
he searched from birth
trying to find a home.

Such a dreadful place
to see suffering like that,
in the trash and waste
where I found orange cat.

As he suffered with broken limb
to not ease his pain
would have been a sin,
so severe was his strain.

Giving him worth and value
I cuddled him in my lap;
providing him affection anew
he loved me for that.

After a hard fought struggle
he died that night.
In the warmth of a cuddle
he ended his plight.

Teacher

I journey in to your mind unknown,
in to your heart of secrets untold.
Where the stitches of your future are sewn,
in to your dreams where your destiny will unfold.

I look deeply and I can see
the extent of your disillusion.
By your side is where I'll be
helping to end your confusion.

For I am your teacher,
a giver of all that I can;
an educator and a nurturer,
committed to helping you I am.

You can completely trust me,
this truth I solemnly say,
for I don't do this for the money,
the love of teaching is why I stay.

Teaching is a gift,
for both the recipient and the giver.
Learning is your precious gift
and mine is being your teacher.

Self-worth isn't about money,
it's about how you live and give.
and I hope there will come a day
when you'll appreciate the teaching I did.

And on that very last day
when I'm called to my final rest,
I'll be comforted in hearing our Lord say,
"Well done teacher, you gave your very best."

Tornado

Feelings of hopelessness
engulf us in a center closet.
We know the warnings
of an eminent tornado.

My family looks to me
in a search for courage
and I try to deliver
by concealing my fears.

I offer assurances
consoling words,
comforting hugs,
and silent prayers.

I know I am helpless
as we await natures wrath
and then it happens -
we all gasp.

The house shakes,
the dogs cling
and fearfully squeal.
The children cry.

..and then – silence, just like that.
It's all over. We survived!
Caring nothing about our losses
we are just grateful to be alive.

Ultimate Fighter

You can't grasp my inner will
to fight the blood sport
where brute force thrives,
power and skill dwell,
and it beacons me by name.

I know this warrior path,
this direction to danger
where the best compete
in the octagon chamber
for the ultimate test.

I hear only silence
in this den of danger
where I deafen my ears
to the cries for blood
amidst yelling cheers.

To be the ultimate fighter,
champion of the best,
is my personal journey,
my defining quest
to discover who I think I am.

Boomers

They were hippies
and societal dropouts.
Scholars, poets and
pot smoking draft dodgers.
Civil right activists,
and anti-war protesters.
Patriots and soldiers
fighting an unpopular war.

Relationships were confused
and marriage became open.
Morality lost meaning and
God was largely forgotten
except to grape Kool-Aid drinkers.
They liked to "groove"
on a Sunday afternoon
and kids hid under desks
for H-bomb drills.

They were good and bad
and pretty and ugly.
They were raised on Dillon,
Joplin, Hendrix and Doors.
Motown was happening
with The Beach Boys, Zeplin,
and the Rollin Stones.
Paul Revere had his Raiders,
Love was a Spoonful and
Three Dog was the Night.
The Beatles reigned supreme.
Sullivan was a king maker,
Elvis was a soldier,
and Archie and Meathead
were "All in the Family."

They welcomed the British invasion
and hung out at Woodstock -
sometimes in the nude.
Many were students
who got high and
routinely cut class.
Most of them were psyche majors
trying to "find themselves?"
LSD was a bad trip
that many took.
Sex was free
and there was a lot of it.

They were spoiled, selfish,
lazy and genius.
They grew up late,
but at least grew up.
They hid their past
and regretted much of it.
They were artistic, clever
and very inventive.
They were also to blame for
much that is wrong.
Many are in denial
and most have regrets.
They were the boomers
of the baby boom generation.

Aye Ireland

Aye Ireland -
king of the ol' plains,
ye beacon us back to
the land of shamrocks,
wid yer pubs-n-ale,
mates and song,
and Celtic traditions
wid Gaelic delight.

Aye Ireland,
on Saint Patty's Day
ye awaken us
to yer majestic beauty,
panoramic shores,
tranquil life,
courageous history
and aye,
yer lovely Irish maidens.

Aye Ireland –
through trails
and tribulation
yer sparkle endures.
Ye embrace faith,
play hard,
laugh hardy
feel yer hearts wid joy
and love
wid deliberation
and purpose.

Aye Ireland –
beautiful Ireland,
king of the ol' plains –
ye beacon us.

bhí dhá labhra budh rí ar seanchlár

Curruption

Debauched, extortionate and inconstant
was the knavish and foul mercenary?
The perfidious praetorian reprobate
was a venal unscrupulous slug.
Debased in character and depraved in spirit
this purveyor of evil tended to his wicked ways.
Morally spoiled, he was a putrid putrescent
and an aberration to integrity.
Nefarious and tainted in character,
he infected the soul.
Treacherous and two-faced,
underhanded and unethical,
debased and unprincipled,
this snide poor excuse to humanity
defined the meaning of "corruption."

Despair

He despaired. He was despondent and desperate.

He was impelled to violent action but restrained from acting out.

He had finally given up. He had lost all hope.

Disheartened and dispirited his will had collapsed.

Lacking confidence or courage, depression defined him.

He languished in gloom and grieved in lament.

He succumbed to a wretched tribulation,

a miserable melancholy, so forlorn was his ordeal.

He anguished over his prospects, so painful was his worry.

Desperate and wholly dejected the criminal faced his judgment.

As justice was served he fretted, ruminated, chafed, sulked and moped.

Now he faced the torment and ridicule he so easily delivered.

Finally, he too understood the meaning of despair.

The Gift of Faith

People ask, "Do you have faith?"
Well, do you?
How do you know?
Do you even know the meaning of faith?

Can you comprehend "obligation?"
Do you understand "loyalty and fidelity"
to a person, promise, engagement, or a diety?
Can you accept the observance of your obligations,
the fidelity to your promises, oaths, and allegiances?
If so, your are blessed with faith.
If not, you are hopelessly devoid of faith's essence.

The value of faith cannot be measured.
It is more precious then any commodity
and cannot be bought nor sold.
If you lack it, faith is only
accessible through prayer.
No one is worthy of faith
and faith is never based on proof.

Faith is a heavenly gift,
a gift from "The Holy Spirit."
It is neither earned or deserved
and ought never be taken for granted.
Faith permits acceptance of our "Lord and Savior"
and HIS "Holy Sacrifice"
that alone can save our souls.

Faith is your connection to the divine.

If you lack faith, pray for it.

If you have faith, cherish it.

In To The Night

In to the night I wondered,
hopelessly looking for that
one hint of truth,
that spiritual essence
that would help me discover
who and what I really am.

Who am I?
What am I?
What should I do?
Who should I be with?
Where should I go
to fully understand my
destiny and purpose in life?

Then, as if succumbed by
glimmering wisdom
it occurred to me;
the journey itself
was the map of truth.
It beckoned the path,
that perfect azimuth
that would lead to the
unsolved mystery of
who and what I really am.

It was only then that I resolved
to relax and enjoy the journey.
It would be a trip through life's
peaks and valley's.
En-route I would witness the
construction of a life time of memories
as I patiently waited for my destiny to unfold

The end of the journey was clouded in mystery
but I sensed its end would come much too soon.
Even if I ventured through more valleys' then peaks
I would still be grateful for having had the opportunity
to take the trip, and I would ultimately cherish
the promised enlightenment that comes only,
in to the night, at journey's end.

Haiku Poetry

LONGING

how i long for you
      the love i epitomize,
who defines my life

CARESS YOUR SOUL

soft and passionate -
      the beautiful touch of love
will caress your soul

AMOUR

a passionate kiss
      titillates sensual bliss
in taboo amour

SACRIFICE

distant warriors
      defending freedom abroad
always sacrifice

TORNADO ALLEY

the tornadoes path
      ran through the central texas
tornado alley

TEXAS STORMS

texas winter storms
      bring treacherous conditions
with freezing ice rain

BLUEBONNET

bluebonnet wildflowers
      are beautiful texas plants
that adorn the countryside

YELLOW ROSE

pretty yellow roses
      are lovely texas flowers
with a pleasing scent

LOST DOG

he lost his tiny dog
      in the thick ceder forest
of wild texas trees

CENTIPEDE

desert centipedes
      are very colorful insects
that you dare not touch

Part II

Short Stories

Simon and Papa John

Simon Gaunt wasn't your average teenager even though his circumstances resembled the experiences of some of the most troubled of youth in modern-day America. Simon was the second oldest of three children. Their father, Henry Gaunt, was an alcoholic who couldn't hold down a job. He deserted his family when Simon was just two years old.

Simon's baby sister Tammy had just been born. Simon's older brother Martin was still just a youngster himself. The responsibility of providing for three children was not in Henry Gaunt's plans. When he left, he never called or visited his family again.

Henry Gaunt did not provide for his family in any way. He didn't even send birthday or Christmas cards much less presents. He was an irresponsible and self-serving bum. He didn't care about his family or anyone else.

Simon's mother, Mary Gaunt, had become pregnant with Mark, Simon's older brother, when she was a16-year old high school student. She dropped out of school to marry Simon's father. Mary believed Henry Gaunt's love proclamations and surrendered her virginity to him while under the influence of some cheap wine. Henry had encouraged her to drink to intoxication.

Mary Gaunt convinced herself that Henry would love and take care of her and their child. She ignored every warning that family and friends tried to tell her. Mary refused to believe that Henry was only interested in sex. Henry reluctantly married Mary only because his parents told him that it was the right thing to do. His parents pressured him to "do the right thing."

Henry Gaunt kept Mary barefoot and pregnant for five years as they survived on welfare, food stamps, and family handouts. He remained unemployed and in a perpetual state of drunkenness the entire time.

When Mary finally had enough and insisted that Henry stop drinking and fulfill his family responsibilities and obligations, out the door he went! Without a high school diploma, Mary Gaunt was forced to work for minimum wage if she could get a job at all. Half the time she was out of work.

Mary tried to provide for her three children as best she could. She understood the huge mistake that she made with her youthful indiscretion. That mistake would define her life, and that of her children, for many years to come. Without an education Mary Gaunt was destined to a life of poverty living in the Five Points area on the East Side of Denver, Colorado.

Five Points was the projects area that most often was referred to as "the slums" or "the ghetto." The area was infested with poor sanitation, rodents, and numerous health hazards. On every corner, one could see alcoholics, drug addicts, prostitutes, and freeloaders. All manner of violence and crime was commonplace daily, especially after nightfall. It was an ugly and dangerous place to live. Still, rent was cheap in these run down and rat infested tenements and it was the only place Mary Gaunt could afford to live as a single parent of three children.

Concerned about what would happen to her children if she lived in "the ghetto" too long, in desperation, Mary turned to prostitution to support her family. Mary Gaunt was an attractive woman. She reasoned that with the money she could earn through prostitution she could save up and move her family out of Five Points.

Mary dreamed about finishing high school and picking up a trade of some kind. She fantasized about someday having a socially acceptable job that would enable her to move her kids out of poverty without her having to sell her body.

Every day before she came home, Mary would pray that God would forgive her for the sinful manner in which she earned her living. Her work filled her with shame and guilt. Mary's parents disowned her. They even turned their back on her children, their own grandchildren, upon learning of Mary's immoral lifestyle. Mary was terrified that her children would also find out that she was a prostitute. She feared losing their love and respect. Sadly, her secret would have to be revealed to them.

Shortly after Simon's 8th birthday, Mary was diagnosed with HIV. Her many liaisons as a prostitute would prove to be fatal. A week before Simon's 12th birthday his mother, whom he dearly loved, died in incredible pain from AIDS.

Now homeless, Simon's grandfather, John Gaunt, whom they lovingly called "Papa John," was the only relative that Simon, Mark, and Tammy could turn to. Papa John happily and lovingly accepted them into his humble home despite the fact that he was poor in health and in wealth.

That hadn't always been the case. Once Papa John had been a true specimen of a man. He was an army paratrooper, a ranger, and a Special Forces intelligence officer. He mastered a variety of martial arts styles while stationed in Japan, Korea, Okinawa and Brazil. Papa John was an accomplished expert in Korean Tae Kwon Do, Okinawa Kaji Kempo, Japanese Sho Do Kan, and Brazilian Ju Jit Su.

Papa John was also a Special Forces master fitness trainer and self-defense instructor. He was not one to boast about his extraordinary physical attributes. He was a humble man, a man of faith.

Only his wife and a few select people knew that that Papa John was the foremost martial artist in the United States Army and perhaps the best in the world. He was so fast and deadly that he could thrust his hand in to a man's chest, pull his heart out, and show it to him before he died. The Special Forces considered Papa John to be a human secret weapon.

Once, while on a secret military mission, Papa John was shot twice while saving the lives of two fellow soldiers. They were being held hostage by terrorists. Papa John killed five of the seven terrorists in hand-to-hand combat, all by himself, prior to being shot.

The two remaining terrorists, upon witnessing what happened to the other five, didn't stick around to see if their bullets had killed Papa John. They were too afraid of Papa John's extraordinary martial arts abilities. Papa John received America's highest award for valor, the Congressional Medal of Honor, for the heroics he displayed on that particular mission.

Few people took notice when the President presented it to him. The citation had to be classified because of the secret nature of the operation. While presenting Papa John with the Medal of Honor, the President openly wept. He said America had never had a more courageous, selfless, and patriotic hero than Papa John.

Sadly, because of the secrecy involved in his military missions, the public could not know about his heroics. Papa John was medically discharged, under honorable conditions. His combat wounds forced his medical retirement. He was provided with a small veteran's disability pension.

Papa John recovered from the bullet wound in his chest but the second bullet logged in his spine. It paralyzed him from the waist down. Beth, his wife, worked as long as she could to help out financially.

Sadly, Beth Gaunt was diagnosed with breast cancer. She died just two years after Papa John's discharge from the army. Papa John was devastated. He loved Beth so deeply that he would never fully recover from her loss.

It was hard for Papa John to go on living. Wheelchair bound, Papa John lived on his small VA pension in a tiny Five Points apartment where a seemingly ungrateful society could care less about his war wounds, heroism, and national service. Only Simon and Tammy, and his deep faith in God, gave him the will to go on.

Time passed by quickly and Martin, Simon's brother, turned 19 while serving a 20-year sentence in the Texas State Prison. He had been convicted of trafficking in illegal drugs and narcotics. Martin Gaunt had already served two terms in a juvenile detention center for possession of illegal drugs, involvement in gang activities, and repeated expulsion from school for poor attendance, failing grades, and a long history of inappropriate behavior.

Unbeknownst to Papa John, Martin had already been involved in drugs and gang activity while his mother was still alive. Martin was a drug addict. He developed his drug addiction through involvement in the East Side Raiders or ESR as they called themselves. ESR was a gang that recruited its members locally. They tried to establish a sort of perverted community bond.

The ESR recruited young. They focused on teenagers who were immature, impressionable, gullible, and easily led. Gang leaders slowly initiated and grew them into the gang. By the time they were old enough and mature enough to understand what they had gotten themselves in to, they had already developed a drug habit and a history of involvement in criminal activities. The gang was like an "evil" family that they needed to feed their out of control drug habits. They also needed to maintain a protective gang shield because rival gangs soon targeted them.

Once in the ESR you were committed for life. You could never quit or leave. The gang, fearful that you would tell what you knew about gang activities, would kill you and even members of your family if you tried to leave the ESR. The ESR was extremely violent.

For its youngest members, the ESR leaders made gang life seem like a brotherhood that looked out for each other. Nothing could be further from the truth. All loyalties were for the ESR, even before family and God. Few members actually believed in God. Those few who did have faith dared not mention God in gang circles.

Papa John was determined not to let Simon and Tammy fall into gang activity and drugs like their older brother Martin did. He decided to teach Simon the many martial arts skills that he himself had mastered. Although Papa John's disability prevented his performing many of the techniques he had mastered, he still had them committed to memory. He still knew how to explain and teach them. Papa John wanted Simon to be able to protect himself and his younger sister.

On his 16th birthday Papa John finally told Simon about his years in clandestine Special Forces operations. The stories intrigued Simon but he wondered if it could all be true. Papa John also showed Simon the Medal of Honor that was given to him for bravery above and beyond the call of duty. Simon admired it even though he didn't understand the medal's full significance.

Papa John made Simon promise to never reveal the secret skills he would teach him. Simon promised to keep the secret and Simon's word was his bond.

Papa John combined social skills and morality lessons, based on his Christian faith, with Simon's martial arts instruction. He taught Simon the evils of drugs, alcohol, and gang activity. He taught Simon that no matter how poor he was he could never justify getting involved in criminal activities. He taught Simon the importance of studying hard and how a good education would be his ticket out of poverty.

Simon listened carefully. He was a very good student. He was also a very good person. Papa John explained that the martial arts were for self-defense and defense of the weak only. He explained how many people fight out of pride and lose their honor as a result. He explained the importance of being non-violent and humble.

Papa John said there was no shame in walking away from a fight. He said that it was dishonorable to stand and fight, out of sheer pride, just so that other people wouldn't think you were a coward. Papa John said, "Doing the right thing is much more important than risking hurting someone or getting hurt yourself, just so others will think that you are a tough guy." He also said, "If there is any means of escape you must leave and even run away before standing and fighting."

Papa John taught Simon to fight only as a last resort when he had no possible means of escape. The only other time fighting was permissible was in defense of the weak or the defenseless. Examples included coming to the aide of an elderly person who was being assaulted, a defenseless woman in peril or a handicapped person being attacked. Papa John made sure that Simon understood and believed these important values before he taught him any of the deadly martial arts skills.

For two years Simon learned the martial arts in secret from Papa John. He learned advanced techniques that were not taught in local karate schools; techniques that were not even known by other martial arts instructors. His training was intense and rigorous. It involved a great deal of conditioning.

Other than school, homework, chores, and church, Simon spent all his remaining hours learning, practicing, and studying martial arts from the world's foremost martial arts master: Papa John.

At the age of 18, Simon had learned everything that Papa John had to teach him. He was even better than Papa John had been in his prime because Papa John also taught Simon how to avoid those few mistakes that he himself had made. Simon was now the most accomplished, the best, and the most dangerous martial artist in the world. But nobody but he and Papa John knew it. That's the way they both wanted it

***

Two weeks after Simon's 18th birthday and eight weeks before he was scheduled to graduate from high school Papa John died of a massive heart attack. He was given a poor man's funeral but with military honors. Simon wanted to do more but this was all that he and Tammy could afford.

With one exception, only Simon, Tammy, a priest and a military honor guard attended Papa John's funeral service. Much to Simon's surprise, an official-looking staff car with four shiny silver stars imbedded in a red plate pulled up to the burial site at the veterans' cemetery where Papa John was being buried. As the bugler played taps the Chairman of the Joint Chiefs of Staff, America's highest ranking general, got out of the staff car and walked up to Papa John's coffin. For several minutes he solemnly stood at attention giving a rigid and respectful hand salute to the coffin where Papa John laid in rest.

Receiving a folded American flag from the honor guard, the general walked up to Simon and said, "I am here representing the President of the United States, myself, the United States Army, and the American people. On behalf of a grateful nation I offer this flag to you in memory of your Papa John, perhaps the greatest secret hero in American history. May he rest in peace." Then the general departed. Simon now knew with certainty that all the stories Papa John had told him were true. He and Tammy cried uncontrollably.

All through school, kids picked on and made fun of Simon. They made fun of his clothes and his shoes. Being so poor, Papa John could only afford to buy second-hand clothes from a local thrift shop. They also made fun of Simon because he studied and received good grades. They called him a geek, a nerd, and a number of other profane names. They called Simon a coward because he would walk and sometimes run from fights.

The so-called good kids would have nothing to do with Simon because he was poor and lived in the bad part of town. They knew Simon's brother was a convicted criminal. Many of them heard the rumors that Simon's mother was a prostitute and that his father was an alcoholic bum who deserted them. They joked about it in pure meanness. Their cruel objective was to offend and upset Simon.

The local gangs, especially the ESR, left Simon alone because they thought he was a coward and weakling. They didn't want to recruit such wimps into their gang. They also knew Simon would have nothing to do with drugs, tobacco, or alcohol. Simon was spit on, tripped, pinched, poked, scratched, bitten, slugged and had objects thrown at him. All he ever did in response was to turn the other cheek and just walk or run away. Simon did this even though he knew that he had the ability to wipe them all out if he really wanted to. Even on those few occasions when Simon became angry enough to fight, he remembered the promise he made to Papa John. Then he would back off, controlling and composing himself. Simon loved and respected Papa John more than anyone. He could never break his promise to him.

Simon and Tammy still lived in Papa John's apartment after he died. One day as Simon approached the apartment he heard a horrifying scream. It was Tammy pleading for someone to help her.

Simon dropped his books and rushed to the apartment door with world-class sprinter speed. The door was locked. Simon yelled "Ki Aii!" Then he leaped into the air and did a turning back kick into the door. His kick landed with such power that the door burst into slivers. The sound of the cracking hard wood door could be heard a block away.

Simon saw three members of the ESR holding his sister. Butch, the gang leader, was unzipping his pants. They were about to gang-rape Tammy. Simon instinctively knew this was one of those rare occasions when fighting was acceptable. He knew that Papa John would approve of his intervening to help his desperate sister.

Simon quickly went into action as Butch called out to the gang members - "Get him!"

The first gang member to reach Simon was the recipient of a flying sidekick into his throat. All one heard was a quick "ugh" sound as his limp body flopped to the floor with blood flowing from his mouth. Two gang members tried to hold Simon as the third attempted to stab Simon with a knife.

Simon did a flip between the two-gang members who were holding his right and left arms and shoulders. This caused them to crash their heads together. They were both knocked out cold. Simon then did a crescent kick with such speed and power that it knocked the knife through the wall while breaking the arm and dislocating the shoulder of the gang member who was holding it.

Then Simon cupped his hands and with lightening speed hit another gang member's ears so hard that the pressure caused his eyes to pop out of his head, blinding him. His pain was agonizing. It was a scary, bloody, ugly sight.

Engulfed in fear and horrified by the lightning speed with which Simon had utterly destroyed four of their fellow gang members, all of whom were known to be big and tough, two of the remaining three ESR gang members jumped out of the nearest window. They jetted away with the speed expected from anyone who genuinely feared for their lives. Both gang members soiled themselves from shear fear and the terror of what they had just witnessed.

Now all that was left was the ESR gang leader Butch. Butch was the biggest, meanest, toughest, and the most feared of any ESR gang member. At six feet and seven inches tall, Butch towered over Simon. He weighed 275 pounds. Every ounce of Butch was solid muscle from many years of heavy bodybuilding and illegal steroid use. His muscles bulged everywhere. When he flexed his shirt split open in the chest and in the arms. It seemed as if his muscles popped out of other muscles. His fists were huge, like fire plugs. He hit like a sledgehammer. As if this were not enough, Butch was also a black belt karate master in his own right.

Butch gritted his teeth. He shouted to Simon, "Prepare to die, punk!" Then Butch lunged forward. It didn't matter. Unbeknownst to Butch he had just picked a fight with Simon Gaunt, grandson and student of Papa John Gaunt. Butch was about to find out that Papa John had trained and developed Simon into the most dangerous man alive.

Simon met Butch with a flurry of reverse punches, chops, and backhands that were so fast that they would have looked like a blur on even a slow-motion camera. In a split second Butch's face looked like it had been through a meat grinder. Blood splattered everywhere. This was followed with a jumping front snap kick, a turning back kick and two roundhouse kicks. All these techniques were delivered with lightning speed.

The final spinning back kick and reverse punch to the side of Butch's face knocked out both rows of his teeth and fractured his skull. The crackling sound of broken bones and body slams could be heard by police approaching from across the street. Tammy had called the police while the fight was in progress.

Butch's entire body flew through the air. His body hit the wall with such force that it imprinted in the wall before it fell to the floor, totally limp, like a huge bag of dead weight potatoes.

As the police ran inside they pulled a gun on Simon. Simon was standing over an unconscious and utterly defeated mass of blood and broken bones previously known as the ESR gang leader Butch.

As Simon was preparing to thrust a final spear hand in to the chest of Butch he paused when hearing the voice of his sister. Tammy cried out, "No Simon! Stop! You're all I have left in this world. Please stop, Simon!"

Simon looked at the police and then at his sister. "Are you alright Tammy?" When she indicated that she was just fine, Simon backed away and said, "Okay, Sis. I won't dishonor you or the memory of Papa John: enough is enough." Simon then held out his hands so the police officer could hand cuff him.

The police officer said, "That won't be necessary, Simon. Your sister explained everything to us. We also caught the two ESR gang members who fled during the fight. They've confessed everything too. It was clearly a matter of self-defense. Thank God you were there to protect your sister. You saved her life Simon. These guys weren't just rapists, they were also killers."

Tammy ran to Simon. She firmly embraced her brother. She cried, hugged, and kissed him on his forehead and cheeks. All the while she cried in relief saying, "Thank you, Simon. Thank you, my dear brother."

***

A rival gang murdered Mark, Simon's older brother, in a prison gang fight. Simon graduated from high school with honors. So did Tammy a year later. Tammy married a doctor. She went on to become a schoolteacher who specialized in working with troubled children. Tammy was very happy and she kept in touch with Simon regularly.

Simon became a Special Forces intelligence officer in the United States Army. He was honored to follow in Papa John's footsteps. Simon was also happily married. He had a son of his own whom he named "Little John," after Papa John.

A lot of kids thought Little John was a bit of a patsy who always ran from fights. One day a neighbor heard a loud "Ki Aii" from behind the privacy fence next door. As he climbed to look over the fence, he saw Simon shaking his finger disapprovingly at Little John.

Little John stood curiously silent with a sorrowful look next to a tree that had just been split in half. There was no ax or saw in sight. ////END////

Big Bertha

They didn't have air conditioning in Central Texas in 1867. August was so hot that a smoky mist seeped from the ground as if the dry cracked soil were perspiring, gasping, and even begging for a cool rain. It was on this burnt ground that the small, one-room rust-painted wooden schoolhouse sat by itself amidst a forest of live oaks, mesquite, and cedar trees. A forest of parched trees that were collectively struggling and clinging to life in the midst of one of the hottest and most unbearable summers in historical memory.

No one would have ever guessed in 1867 that this same ground would one day be the home of a thriving city of over 100,000 citizens known as Killeen. It would also host the largest and most sophisticated military installation in the world: Fort Hood, Texas.

The tiny schoolhouse crammed in seventeen students ranging between 6 and 16 years of age. 1st through 10th grade were taught in one room by a single teacher. Few students stayed past the 8th grade. No students went beyond 10th grade. Teenagers were part of the much-needed agricultural labor pool. Their labor was needed on the farms and in the forests.

Miss Warlock, also known as Big Bertha, taught all the students. Bertha Warlock had a very strange family history. Legend has it that she was the daughter of Gertrude Warlock, a wicked witch. She had cast a spell on Allen Warlock, Big Bertha's father. This spell caused Allen Warlock to fall in love with Gertrude. The wicked witch Gertrude was decrepit and vile-looking. She had squinty gray eyes; bushy eyebrows; large ears; a cleft, protruding chin; and rotting teeth.

Even so, the spell she cast on the trapper Allen Warlock made Gertrude appear beautiful to him. While under her spell Allen asked Gertrude the witch to be his bride. They quickly married on January 1, 1868. Ten months later on Halloween night, October 31, 1868, the wicked witch Gertrude gave birth to a very large and an unusually ugly baby girl. She named the baby Bertha. This baby would grow up to be the legendary Big Bertha.

After two years, Gertrude's evil spell wore off Allen Warlock. He was finally able to see the wretched witch that he married while under her evil spell. The sight of her was so shocking that Allen Warlock almost succumbed to heart failure. It took him months to recover and even then it was not a full recovery.

The thought of having to spend the rest of his life with such a wicked wife filled Allen Warlock with despair. He lost his will to live. The end finally came when Gertrude forced her affections on Allen. He was bedridden and defenseless. Allen tried to fight her off but his brave attempt was no match for Gertrude's evil magic. She placed yet another spell on him.

This spell forced Allen Warlock to hold his breath until he fainted into unconsciousness. He died soon thereafter. The final cause of his death was the subject of much speculation over the years. Most believed that Gertrude murdered her husband while he was in his unconscious trance. Others thought he died from another heart attack while being forced to hold his breath under Gertrude's evil spell.

The truth remains a mystery to this day. Whatever the actual cause of death was, heart attack or murder, nobody disputed the fact that Gertrude's evil spell lead to her husband's death in some manner.

It was common knowledge during this period that Allen had nothing to do with his daughter Bertha. At the time of his death, Bertha was only one year old. Even at this young toddler's age, Bertha was mysterious and overpowering. Her father was afraid of her. The normal father-daughter bonding never developed between them.

Bertha was known to dislike males of all ages. She avoided the company of boys and men whenever possible, unless she had some particular use for them. Some of the boys and men whom Bertha came in contact with mysteriously vanished. They were never heard from again. No one knew why. It was widely believed that Gertrude the witch was teaching her daughter, Bertha, to hate men even at this tender young age.

The circumstances surrounding Allen Warlock's death became public on the second anniversary of his death. Human bones were found around an outdoor barbecue pit next to the log cabin of Gertrude the witch. A rawhide identification wristband identified the remains as being that of Allen Warlock.

Within days of this discovery, Gertrude Warlock was tried and convicted for murder and cannibalism. The evidence proved that Gertrude had barbecued the remains of her husband. Afterwards she ate his flesh. It is not known if her daughter Bertha shared in this feast of human remains.

Since Gertrude Warlock had been convicted of witchcraft, sorcery, murder, and cannibalism, she was sentenced to death and burned alive at the stake. A single newspaper report of the execution was discovered many decades latter. It was the only record of what took place that day. This report reflected eyewitness accounts of Gertrude the witch laughing as her flesh burned. It was as if she felt no pain. Her eyes were reported to have turned crimson red. It said her head turned slowly from left to right with an evil and chilling glare.

Seconds before dying, Gertrude shrieked out a warning. She said, "Beware, my magic will live in my other flesh. I shall return and gain my revenge on man."

Up to this point her skin and flesh only peeled under the heat of the intense flames. Then suddenly it turned to ash and vanished in a mysterious manner.

It is uncertain what Gertrude meant about returning in her other flesh. Most folks believed she was referring to her daughter Bertha who was, of course, of her flesh. From that day forward Bertha was held highly suspect. She was avoided by practically everyone.

Bertha Warlock, or Big Bertha, thus lost both her parents at a very young age. Ordinarily this would be a tragedy but in Big Bertha's case it was a blessing in disguise. The police investigated further and discovered the skeletal remains of 27 missing children buried near Gertrude's cabin. Gertrude the witch had placed spells on them.

These spells put the children in a trance whereupon Gertrude would kill and eat them. Afterwards she would bury the remains. Had Gertrude not been executed she might have killed and eaten her own daughter, the legendary Big Bertha. The prevailing concern at the time was that the blood of Gertrude ran through Big Bertha's veins. Many feared that Big Bertha would become like her mother.

Grandma Warlock, Big Bertha's paternal grandmother, raised her granddaughter - Bertha. Grandma Warlock was a good and kind person. She tried her best to teach Bertha good values and the importance of getting a good education. Bertha studied hard and earned excellent grades. Other than chores she did nothing else but study. Bertha tried to make friends at an early age but was always rejected. Everyone associated her with Gertrude, her witch mother. Parents did not permit their children to play with or associate with Bertha. The boys teased her and the girls made fun of her.

Bertha quickly became bitter and angry. She learned to hate boys and lost interest in making friends with other girls. She became a complete outsider. She was a loner. Bertha didn't fit in with anyone. She often talked to herself or so it seemed. It was as if she were somehow communicating with her long dead mother, Gertrude the witch.

On occasion Bertha was seen mixing potions waving her hands over them in a mysterious way. When questioned, she said she was learning to cook and that she was reciting recipes to herself. Was it cooking or was it witch's sorcery as many believed? Nobody really knew for sure.

Bertha grew much faster than other children her age. By the time she was 14 Bertha had already reached a height of 6 feet 2 inches. She weighed over 200 pounds. By her 20th birthday Bertha had matured in to a 6 foot 7 inch 325-pound woman. She had very little body fat. Bertha was as solid as a rock.

Occasionally Bertha would have disagreements with some of the tough loggers and trappers in the area. This happened only when she went shopping in town for her grandmother. Feeling the effects of too much whiskey the loggers sometimes teased Bertha about her unusual size and her homely looks. Bertha usually just turned her back and walked away from them.

However, if they brought up Gertrude, Bertha's witch mother, she would lose control. A fight would break out that was a spectacle to witness. Not once did a logger or trapper walk away from a fight with Big Bertha. She would pound them unconscious. Her hammer fist was as powerful as a sledgehammer. She smashed it against the side of the face and other body parts of anyone who challenged her.

Some did not survive the fight. Since these fights were always witnessed and because Bertha acted in self-defense, she never faced criminal charges. Those who survived a Big Bertha beating were never the same again. You could spot her victims a mile away. They were the crippled remains of once gallant and strong men. Their deformed, twisted, mangled and disabled bodies were unsightly and pitiful looking. They begged considerable compassion from onlookers.

Bertha Warlock's exceptional grades earned her a full scholarship to the University of Texas. It was there that she set out to fulfill her life's ambition of becoming a teacher.

There are no records that speak to what transpired until August 28th, 1892. Big Bertha was 24 years old at the time. She had just accepted the teaching position in the rusty-colored, one-room country school in Bell County, Central Texas. She was the only teacher in the school.

The land upon which this school was built would some day be near the center of a city that would become known as Killeen, Texas. This fact would later prove to be significant. The record is very sketchy after this, except that it is known that a few influential locals tried to fire Big Bertha from her teaching position. Their reasons for wanting to fire her remain sketchy. However legend has it that they were acting on a popular public appeal.

Their efforts to fire Big Bertha failed. There is no record of why it failed. It is only known that two of the five men who sought her dismissal mysteriously disappeared. The other three, the brothers Clyde and Jethro Belton and their cousin Jessie Stillhouse were in a complete state of shock. They had witnessed or been subjected to something awful. They could not be persuaded to speak about what transpired, not even when threatened with death, so great was their fear.

Big Bertha's name was perpetuated by her students because of her enormous size, strength, and what seemed like her supernatural powers. It is known that Big Bertha remained a spinster, having never married. She did not like men. She could also be ruthless with women if they crossed her. Big Bertha lived alone and remained a loner her entire life. She would go into violent rages if anybody disturbed her peace.

Big Bertha was known to be an excellent teacher. She was also extremely tough. She could be a mean and ruthless disciplinarian. Big Bertha was usually nice to students who tried their best, received passing grades, and who demonstrated good behavior.

However, Big Bertha was mean and ruthless with poor students who demonstrated bad behavior. She built her own paddle. The students nicknamed the paddle the "butt buster." The butt buster was 18 inches long and 18 inches wide. It was 3 inches thick. It had 21 small holes and 21 metal welts screwed into it. Just three swats with the butt buster left a student crying in agony. It always left bruises, blisters, and welts on their behinds. One could hardly survive more than four swats with the butt buster. The students quickly learned: *Don't mess with Big Bertha.*

Big Bertha was so strong she could pick up the largest kid in the class, with one hand, by the back of his neck. She could lift him completely off the ground while swatting him with the butt buster using her other hand. Even the older teenagers would cry and beg for mercy when someone was being punished by Big Bertha. Not many students dared to screw up in Big Bertha's class. If they did it was only once.

They made sure never to get her angry again. She was downright scary and she always inflicted great pain on badly behaved students.

At the age of 57 Big Bertha suffered a severe heart attack and died. She had no living relatives. The local officials decided to bury Big Bertha in the back of the old wooden school house. They placed a simple wooden marker over her grave. The grave marker read, *Here lies the best, meanest, and toughest teacher that ever lived— Big Bertha.* Nothing more needed to be added to the marker. Her legend spoke for itself.

With all the mystery and suspicion surrounding Big Bertha, she was always considered to be an outstanding teacher. Her students always did better academically than their peers. In adult life her former students usually became more wealthy and successful. Their success was largely credited to Big Bertha's exceptional teaching skills.

Big Bertha thought of her students as family in a perverted sort of way. This was because she had no living relatives. Being buried by the schoolhouse was indeed a great tribute and memorial to her. It was the one place that she could most rest in peace assuming, of course, that nobody ever disrupted her peaceful rest.

Two years after Big Bertha's death lighting struck the old wooden school house. It burned the school and Big Bertha's grave marker to the ground. Soon thereafter another school was built in a new location several miles away.

Trees, brush, and grass grew over the area of the old wooden school house and Big Bertha's grave. Because her grave was no longer marked it was forgotten about within a decade.

About a century after Big Bertha's death the city of Killeen had grown and thrived in Central Texas. It was overrun with students. In 1994 a new school, Brookhaven, was built on the exact spot where Big Bertha was buried. Nobody realized that her grave was still there because no marker identified the gravesite.

Just prior to opening the new Brookhaven School a routine check was made with the city graves registration. Only then did they discover that the southwest corner of the Brookhaven School had been built over Big Bertha's grave. City and school district officials met to decide what should be done. It was decided that it would be prohibitively expensive to tear down the school and move the grave. That plainly was not an option.

Since Big Bertha had no living relatives and only a few people knew her grave existed, they decided to do nothing at all. They acted as if it hadn't happened. This would prove to be a frightening mistake.

After the Brookhaven School opened, the school's custodians started to complain. They were concerned about some very strange happenings that occurred while they were cleaning the school after dark. There was talk of eerie noises, unexplained flying objects, and just plain spooky events.

Brookhaven experienced a large turnover of custodian personnel. The custodians were quitting almost as fast as they were hired. They told anyone who would listen about the spooky events but nobody believed them. Nothing ever happened during the day when the students and teachers were there. Hence, the authorities assumed the spooky stories were being made up by disgruntled employees, the custodians.

About five months into the school year Brookhaven started a Behavior Management class for students who were having difficulty with their behavior. These students were occasionally required to stay after school for several hours because of poor behavior. This was called after school intervention but the students themselves called it *late night*.

It was when these students stayed for *late night* that the authorities finally found out what was really going on. They quickly learned that the custodians had been honest about their spooky encounters.

Recall that legend said Big Bertha was tough and sometimes ruthless with badly behaved students. They were students much like those who had to stay for *late night* in modern times. It turns out that when they built the Brookhaven School over Big Bertha's gave the construction disrupted her peaceful rest. Big Bertha's spirit came to life. Her ghost started haunting the Brookhaven School. She would never come out of her grave during daylight hours. That is why none of the students or staff who were at Brookhaven during daylight hours saw or heard her. Big Bertha's ghost was only active after darkness fell. This explains why the custodians experienced all the strange and spooky happenings at night.

Big Bertha's activities could be heard but she would rarely show herself unless bad students were in the school or on school property. Her ghost usually remained indoors, in the southwest corner of the school, near her grave. However, on occasion her ghost would fly to other parts of the school. Sometimes she would go outside on school grounds. It was as if she were protecting her turf.

Big Bertha's ghost was off-white, almost creamy in color. It was also transparent in that you could see through parts of it as if looking through a hazy cloud like substance. Her hair was pure white. It was shoulder length and was parted in the middle. Her eyes were big, round, and pitch black. Big Bertha's ghost still wore her long white burial dress. It had ruffles around the neck, the bottom of the dress and around the wrists of her long sleeves.

Big Bertha's nose was very wide and long. Her cheeks were full and rotund. She had a large mole near her square and dimpled chin. Her lips were full and pale. Her mouth was wide. She had a few missing teeth. Those teeth that remained were large, pointed, and sharp. Her fingernails were also long and pointed. They resembled the claws of a wild beast.

When Big Bertha appeared she hovered in mid-air. She slowly turned her head from left to right. She glared in each direction. It was very eerie. When she saw a bad kid, Big Bertha would let out a high pitch screeching scream. It was a kind of "eeyeee" sound. Big Bertha's ghost could look at objects such as trash cans, desks, and chairs and with mind control could send them flying through the air at a high speed. Sometimes she would intentionally miss the student, intending only to scare him or her. That was what she usually did to misbehaved female students.

Recall that Big Bertha was much tougher on male students than female students. Most often, if it were a boy, she would let the object hit him. For the worst behaved students the butt buster would magically appear. Big Bertha would levitate the student as if picking him up by the back of the neck. Then she would attack him with the butt buster. These students ether died from the whopping or ended up in the hospital badly beaten up and in excruciating pain.

On one occasion two teachers tried to come to the aide of a couple of students. Big Bertha, who usually left teachers alone, became very angry when they tried to interfere. She levitated the largest teacher, who weighed over 265 pounds, and threw him into the other teacher. They both crashed against the wall with considerable force.

The smaller teacher was crushed to death. Being hit with the velocity and force of the larger teacher that came flying through the air was more then the smaller teacher's body could endure. The larger teacher ended up with a broken back. Big Bertha's ghost levitated over him for a few seconds. She waved her index finger back and forth at the suffering big teacher. It was as if she were trying to say "naughty naughty, don't ever do that again." Then she vanished.

Several students, parents, teachers and other staff have seen the ghost of Big Bertha. over the years. All the sightings have been at night and especially on Halloween. Recall that Halloween is the anniversary of both Big Bertha's birth and her death. Each year on Halloween many teenagers converge on the Brookhaven School hoping to see Big Bertha and to demonstrate their courage. Many of them have lived to regret it. Some times Big Bertha appears and sometimes she doesn't. When she does appear it is always an unforgettable and frightening experience.

Most people who have seen Big Bertha elect not to talk about it. They fear that nobody will believe them. Others, out of concern that the Brookhaven students might become alarmed or that parents will worry, elect to deny the existence of Big Bertha. They frequently tried to end her legendary story but the Legend of Big Bertha lives on.

What do you believe? If you are in doubt someday you might see Big Bertha yourself. If you do, for your sake, I hope that you have been a good student. Always remember to stay away from the Brookhaven School on Halloween. The ghost of Big Bertha will make a believer out of anyone.   ////END////

David's Angel

David watched her walk down the hall, first from the front as she entered the school building and then from behind as she passed his wall locker. Her name was Janet. She took David's breath way. Her hair was shiny and soft. It was dark brown and shoulder length. It bounced off her shoulders as she walked. Her sky blue eyes radiated against her tanned olive complexion.

Janet's skin was as smooth as silk. Her teeth were perfect and pearly white. Her smile captivated all on-lookers. Her figure was total perfection. She walked with a gait that resembled professional fashion models. Janet wasn't just beautiful; she was the essence of beauty. David fantasized about her warm embrace. He visualized sharing a warm kiss of passion from her soft shapely lips.

Fantasizing was all that David could do because Janet wouldn't have anything to do with him. She wouldn't even offer him the simple kindness of a friendly nod; not even the courtesy of sharing the time of day with him.

Unfortunately, Janet's personality didn't match her spectacular looks. She may have been the most beautiful girl in school, but she was also the most conceited and one of the cruelest students imaginable. She was very selective in whom she dated. If a fellow wasn't a handsome jock athlete with finely toned hard body muscles, and who drove a spectacular car and had plenty of cash to spend, he could just forget about ever dating Janet. In fact, he could forget about her even acknowledging him unless he was the targeted recipient of one of her many put downs.

David didn't understand this situation when he arrived at Cove High School. He rightfully considered himself to be a good, decent, honest, and hard working individual. As such, he felt somewhat comfortable in asking a pretty girl like Janet out on a date.

In the back of his mind David was aware of his noticeable blemishes — his pimpled face and his chubby physique. He was self-conscious about this. Still, he viewed his recent move to Texas, a new school, and making new friends as the new beginning he sought. David was much more upbeat and confident then he had ever been before. His intentions were honorable.

David just wanted the pleasure of enjoying Janet's company. He was hopeful that he might gain the comfort of getting to know a popular girl in his new school. He figured it would be worth the risk of rejection to ask Janet out on a date. Perhaps, he thought, she could help him to be accepted by the other students who didn't easily welcome newcomers in to their ranks.

David arrived at Cove High just in time for the school prom. His father was in the Army. They had just returned from a tour of duty in Germany. David was really excited and happy to be back in the good ol' USA. This was his home and he had missed it.

David had been harassed and bullied by his peers in Germany. He was anxious to get away from that situation. Most tragic of all, David was still mourning the death of Becky, his twin sister. She had died two years before. A drunk driver ran in to her when she was walking home from school. Her death devastated David. Becky wasn't only his sister; she was his best friend and confidant. They loved each other unconditionally.

David didn't know a soul in his new central Texas home. He desperately wanted to make friends and to be accepted in his new school. It took considerable courage for David to ask Janet to be his prom date. However, after several days he was finally able to summon up the courage to ask her. David approached Janet at her wall locker just after lunch. It was a week before the prom.

After David asked her to the prom Janet smiled at David with a devilish grin. Then she said, "Hey girls, come over here. I want you all to witness this prom date offer."

Janet was the captain of the cheer leading squad and all the cheerleaders came running over on her command. When all the cheerleaders had gathered around Janet said, "O.K., Dude, ask me in front of witnesses."

With a clear mind David ordinarily would have been able to figure out that something unpleasant was about to happen. However, his mind was anything but clear at this emotional moment. Not understanding, David smiled at Janet and said, "Janet, I find you to be more than attractive. I think you are absolutely beautiful. I would be honored if you would accept my invitation. Please be my date to the school prom."

Led by Janet, all the cheerleaders and everyone else within hearing distance burst into uproarious laughter. Once they had quieted down Janet said, "Are you completely nuts? How dare you ask me out on a date you pimple-faced, fat, pudgy midget! When God was handing out good looks to the babies in pregnant women your mother must have been on a drunken binge. She probably did a belly flop into a mud hole. Get real you ugly jerk! Not only would I never go out with you, you're going to have to answer to Ralph. Ralph is my boyfriend. He's not going to be happy when he finds out you tried to hit on me."

David was shattered, devastated, and heart broken. He had suffered embarrassment before but never with such public humiliation. It was hard enough being the new kid, not knowing a soul, and not having any friends; but for this to happen, for someone to be so totally mean just because he dared to ask her to the prom was — well, it was hurtful beyond expression.

David walked briskly away from Janet and the crowd of onlookers. He turned his head in his best effort to conceal the tears that were now welling up in his eyes. He didn't want anyone to see him cry. He knew they would ridicule him if they caught a glimpse of his tears.

David got on his bike. He began pedaling as fast as he could. David's father was a junior enlisted soldier and his family couldn't afford much. They had a single inexpensive second-hand car. David hadn't even learned how to drive yet. He figured, "why bother?" He knew it would be years before he could afford a car of his own. His bicycle was a Christmas present from his grandparents. He cherished it. David was trying to get home and out of sight as fast as he possibly could. He lived four miles from school. He rode his bike back and forth to school every day.

David rounded a curve pedaling at a fast rate of speed. He was on the down hill side of a steep street. Suddenly a flashy hemi-powered quad-cab Ram 1500 truck pulled up behind him. It began honking its horn.

David pulled to the right side of the road. He wanted to make sure the truck had plenty of room to pass. The truck did not pass. It stayed right behind David. The driver continued to honk his horn. The other occupants joined the driver in laughing and shouting obscenities at David.

Finally, as if out of nowhere and for no reason, the truck nudged David's bike with its bumper. At these high speeds, that is all that it took to send David flying through the air. He landed head first, in the gravel at the roadside.

The truck stopped and Ralph, Janet's boyfriend, emerged from the drivers' seat. He and the other hooligan occupants walked over to David. David, nearly unconscious, was lying in severe pain in the gravel and dirt.

Ralph was an all-state linebacker on the high school football team. He stood towering over David. He grinned as he looked down at David. David was a pitiful site. He was bruised and scratched everywhere on his body. His right arm and leg and several ribs were broken. His skull was fractured and he had internal bleeding. Half dazed, it was all David could do just to look up at Ralph. He had a helpless look of bewilderment that was evident even in his swollen and disfigured face.

The six-foot five-inch and 275-pound linebacker Ralph was carrying a tire iron. Ralph said, "I'll teach you to hit on my woman — you freaking little wimp."

Before David had the opportunity to say that he had no way of knowing that Janet even had a boyfriend, Ralph began to club David with the tire iron. He did this in a mad frenzy. Ralph's football buddies who, like Ralph, were supposed to be positive role models, instead joined in on the beating. They kicked David in every part of his body.

When it was clear that David was fully unconscious and appeared lifeless, Ralph and his buddies got back in the truck and drove away. David was left bleeding profusely. He was totally unrecognizable. His face was completely disfigured. David just lay there, nearly dead, until a passerby noticed him. The passerby called the 911 emergency line on his cell phone. Within minutes an ambulance and the police arrived.

David's mother was the first to arrive at the hospital emergency room. His father was out of state on a field training exercise. He couldn't be reached. Medical personnel were working frantically to stabilize David. His condition had been labeled critical.

David slowly turned his head to look at his mother. His eyes were sad and tear filled. In a weak and whispered voice David asked, "Why Mom? Why am I so ugly?" He was gasping between words.

David's mother tried to compose herself and appear brave for her son. Inside, she was trembling with fear. It was obvious to her that David's condition was extremely serious. It was a struggle for her to hold back her tears.

"Why am I short and fat? Why can't I make friends Mom? Why doesn't anyone like me?"

David's mother clenched his hand. She tried to think of a comforting response but her mind was confused. She was overcome by sorrow and grief. No mother should ever have to see her child in this condition. It was almost unbearable.

With an even weaker whisper, David asked, "Why did God take Becky away? She is the only one who ever talked to me. She cared about me. I miss her Mom. I need her. I want to be with Becky. I'm sorry Mom; I don't care anymore. I've had enough heartache."

David's mother, half demanding and half begging, cried out, "You hold on David! Don't you dare die on me."

In little more then a weak whisper David said, "Mom, maybe I will finally find peace and happiness in death."

No longer able to control her emotions and wholly succumbing to tears, David's mother fully embraced her son in a nurturing embrace.

"David, in God's eyes and in mine, you are a beautiful person. He knows how good a person you have grown to be. He knows that you did nothing wrong. You did not deserve to have this happen to you. God loves you David. So do Dad and me. Please David, be strong. Hold on my son."

Wiping tears from her eyes she stroked David's hair and gently kissed his forehead. "Please son," she said, "Talk no more. You're very weak. You need to save your strength. Please rest while the doctors attend to you."

"But Mom, maawuum." David gasped. Suddenly his eyes went blurry. Then they rolled back in his head. His whole body went limp.

David's mother cried out, "Dear God — please help my son!! Doctors, hurry! You've just got to save him!"

The nurses quickly ushered David's mother out of the emergency room. The doctors hurriedly went in to all manner of life saving procedures. Then, a buzzing sound came from the machine that David was attached to. The same sound that indicates heart failure.

As a nurse pulled a sheet over David's head, a doctor went out to his mother. With heartfelt compassion he told her, "Ma'am, I'm so very sorry. We did all we could do."

David's mother collapsed into the doctor's arms. The shock; the despair and grief were too agonizing for her to endure.

David was the nicest and kindest son that any parent could hope to have. He was a good student. He did his chores without complaining. He volunteered at church and for other community projects. David would give anyone the shirt off his back if he thought they needed it. He would even do it if they just wanted it and he believed that giving it to them would make them happy.

Although nobody wanted to be his friend, David never stopped trying to be friendly to everyone that he met. David loved everyone. He was just a loving kind of guy. He even loved those who ridiculed and harmed him. He would occasionally get angry, like everyone else, but he didn't know how to hold a grudge. He couldn't be vindictive or vengeful. He didn't want to learn how to either. One had to wonder how this could happen to a wonderful person like David.

* * *

Meanwhile, back in the emergency room, David was levitating. He was floating in mid-air above his bed. He was curiously looking at himself lying there with a sheet over his head. David was able to see and hear everything that was going on, but nobody could see him.

At first David couldn't understand why his body wasn't moving or why his pain had left him. Then, as if out of nowhere, a bright light appeared. Out of that light a warm hand reached out to David. Then a full radiant angelic figure appeared.

"Who are you?" David asked.

"I am Elijah. I am your guardian angel, David. I have always been with you."

Then another light appeared. Out of it came a beaming teenage girl. David cried out, "Becky! Becky! Is that you Becky? Can it really be...?" Then he paused to think. "Oh my God Becky, if I can see you than I must also be dead."

"My dear brother," Becky answered, "Listen carefully to Elijah. I want you to know that I'm all right. I'm even better than all right. I am happy and at peace here. I've been with grandma, grandpa, and Uncle Joe. They are happy and at peace as well. They send their love. You may come and join us when it is your time, but not a moment sooner. God must choose the time and place David, not you."

"Becky, I have so many questions."

"In due time all your questions will be answered, but not now."

"When Becky? When is the right time?

"That is God's decision, David. Elijah will explain all you need to know for now."

"But Becky, please…"

Becky motioned David to silence.

"I can't stay any longer David. I can't say any more either. Please tell Mom and Dad what you saw and tell them I love them. Remember David, I love you, too." Then Becky vanished.

"Don't worry David," Elijah said. "When your time comes you will be with Becky in heaven as she is now with you in spirit."

"Then why am I here now?"

"Because God has been speaking to you, David. You haven't been listening. You haven't paid attention."

"I don't mean to be disrespectful Elijah but I don't understand what you mean."

"David, as you have already experienced, God has taken some rather drastic measures to get your attention."

"Yes, I guess I'd have to agree that this is rather drastic. But why…?"

"Patience David. What you need to know you will know, but nothing more."

"Is all the suffering that I have had to endure going to be explained? What about the beating that I just suffered? Why did that happen? Was that part of God's drastic measures for me?"

"No David. God doesn't do evil things but there is evil in the world in which you live. Sometimes bad things happen to good people"

Now more confused than ever David wondered why God allowed bad people to hurt good people. After all, David thought to himself, "God can do anything so why not protect the innocent from being harmed by those who are evil?"

Elijah read David's mind. Before David could ask another question Elijah offered an explanation.

"David, God gave each of us free will. He could have ordained that everyone do exactly what He wanted because, after all, He is God. However, that was not what God wanted. He wanted us to love and obey Him rather then compelling us to do so.

Free will was the only way that we ourselves could voluntarily give God what He wanted."

"Wow! I never thought about it that way before Elijah."

"David, free will also means that bad people can choose to do bad things to good people. If God intervened He would be taking away the free will of those people. The whole purpose of free will is so that everyone can choose to be good or bad."

"But Elijah, wouldn't good come out of His intervening?"

"Think about it David, free will is a divine decision. If God intervened then He would be a liar. Because God is perfect, He cannot lie. He will intervene in response to prayers but He won't take away anyone's free will."

"What about you, Elijah? You said you were my guardian angel. Shouldn't you have been guarding — you know, protecting me?"

"I was protecting, David. I always have been in a spiritual way."

"Spiritual way?"

"You see David, I am bound to do the Lord's will for you, not your will for yourself. My job is not to protect you from the rigors of living in your earthly world. If that were the case nobody would ever suffer any hardship because everyone is given a guardian angel. I am charged with helping to guide you away from sinfulness.

"Then why am I a sinner? What happened to your guidance?"

"Unfortunately sin is a manifestation of the world in which you live. You just have to keep recognizing it, fighting it, and seek forgiveness whenever you discover it in yourself."

"As my guardian angel can't you advise and worn me before I fall in to sin?"

"I try to persuade and influence you David but I do not dictate your thoughts or actions. If I did it would be interfering with your God-given free will."

"I never heard you. How did you persuade and influence me?"

"I am your conscience. Listen to your conscience and you will hear me."

"Is that what you meant when you said I haven't been paying attention to God?"

"Exactly!"

"Is that it? That's the whole message I'm supposed to hear?"

"It's a profoundly important message David but there is a little more."

"I'm listening."

"David, do you remember when you talked about being ugly? How you complained about your pimpled face, your fat pudgy body and what you perceived to be your overall bad looks?"

"Well yes. I guess I do remember that."

"You see David, the love of physical appearance is a prideful kind of sin. Love has nothing to do with good looks."

Elijah allowed David to reflect on that for a moment and then he continued.

"Real love isn't something you see David; it's something that you feel. You passed judgment on yourself David. You did this based on the hurtful and sometimes evil opinions of others. You have no right to judge anyone and that includes yourself. Only God can judge man! How could you think that God failed to love you just as you are? After all, you are His creation. God doesn't make junk!"

"Elijah, I feel just terrible. I never understood this before."

"David, do you honestly believe that God was not pleased with His creation in you? He made you exactly the way He wanted for His own reasons. Those reasons have absolutely nothing to do with what others think. His creation is perfect even if it appears flawed to the eyes of those who are imperfect in thought. Understand David, in heaven there is no such thing as an ugly person."

"I'm so sorry, Elijah? Will God forgive me?"

Elijah smiled. "Of course he will David. Just ask his forgiveness and repent. Try to learn from your mistakes and not repeat them. Then you will receive His forgiveness.

"Is their anything else?"

"You've just been enlightened David. You were chosen for this enlightenment. That is a special blessing David. The understanding of these messages will profoundly impact on your life and those you share this message with. Be grateful.
"

"I am grateful Elijah. I truly am. Thank you"

"David, you've also been blessed by your having seen the pathway to heaven. It means you have the Lord's favor. But heaven itself must wait."

"Can I at least see Heaven now?"

"As Becky said, God must pick the time and place. If you could see heaven now you would never want to return. Heaven is so beautiful and magnificent that life in your world could never compare. Having to return would leave you in such despair that you might sin to get back. That sin would lead you away from heaven. God can not lead you in to sin nor can he punish you for sin if He caused you to sin. That would invalidate His divinity which is impossible. Sin is always a personal choice David. It can never be derived from our Lord and Savior, from our God. No David, you've seen the path to heaven but the door must remain closed to you for the time being."

"But what if I want to go there now and stay with Becky? I mean I'm not really happy where I am now."

"David, David. Please pay attention. Heaven is your final reward. It's the most precious gift you will ever receive and it's an eternal gift?'

..And?"

"The point is that it is a *gift* from God. You can't just take it or demand it because then it would no longer be a *gift*. You can't get in to heaven that way. There is only one way David, and only one path."

"..And the right way, the path is?"

"Through Jesus. He is the way, the truth, and the light. That's the most important message I have for you David. Do you understand?"

"Yes Elijah. I understand. ..and I will also share that message with others."

"Good David. Very good. Remember, God knows best. Also remember that I am with you always."

With those final words, Elijah faded away.

* * *

Suddenly a nurse screamed out in the emergency room, "Doctor! Doctor! Come quickly!"

The doctor rushed in just in time to see David move. Only moments before he had personally pronounced David dead. First his fingers moved. Then his hands and arms moved. Then he moved from side-to-side. He was moaning but David was very much alive.

"How can this be?" the doctor said. "I don't understand. I'm certain. I double checked! David's heart had clearly stopped beating. He stopped breathing. It was unmistakable. David was dead. Yet, now he lives. How can this be?"

Just then David's mother came running into the room. Embracing her son she cried out, "Thank you Lord! Thank you for answering my prayers."

An observant nurse said to the doctor, "What you have just witnessed is a genuine miracle doctor. A God given miracle."

Ralph and his buddies were tried as adults under Texas law. They were convicted of attempted murder. Each of them was sentenced to 15 years in State prison. Janet was convicted for conspiracy to commit murder. She was sentenced to 10 years in the State women's prison. These sentences were reduced to supervised probation at the personal request of David.

Acting in the compassionate likeness of Jesus who said "Father forgive them for they know not what they do," David asked the judge to be compassionate with his attackers. David forgave them unconditionally. This extreme act of kindness changed all their lives forever more. They all were genuinely grateful and went on to become good, kind, caring and compassionate citizens. They, like David, became a blessing to others.

David graduated from high school with honors. Fully understanding his calling, his mission, he went on to college and than became a youth minister. David specialized in helping children with low self-esteem.

David fell in love with and went on to marry a beautiful woman. She loved David for the content of his character. David was happy. More importantly he discovered that he had a gift for making other people happy.

Every night when David went to bed, before he fell asleep, he would say his ritual prayers. He thanked God for the wonderful life that he had. David always concluded his prayer by saying, "Elijah, I know you're there. Thank you Elijah. Good night."
////END////

Ed Coet – "The Poet Coet"

Ed Coet, B.S., M.A., is also known to his many fans as "The Poet Coet." Ed Coet is a retired US Army officer and a decorated and partially disabled combat veteran. Many of Ed's poems reflect his love of country and his military background. His strong devotion and commitment to faith and family and his keen interest in introspective thought are also reflected in many of Ed's poems.

Ed Coet is also a retired professional educator. He is certified in both special education and generic general education. Ed has taught elementary through high school and has been writing poetry for decades. He began writing short stories for his students in Central Texas. His students liked the stories and poems so much that Ed, with his students' encouragement, began writing for publication. The rest is history.

Ed Coet is currently the editor of the Blue Fog Journal. He is now a widely published and highly respected freelance writer and poet. His numerous columns and articles on a variety of topics have been published in newspapers, magazines, ezines and blogs throughout the United States and abroad. His short stories and poems have been published in over 30 magazines, ezines, and journals in the United States, Great Britain, Canada, Fiji, India, and South Africa. Ed Coet's anthology credits include Namaste Fiji – The International Anthology of Poetry Book, The "Breaking Silences" Poetry Book Collection, and the 2007 Scars Poetry Collection Book - We The Poet's, which includes his award-winning poem – Comfort. More recently Ed Coet's poems were published in the poetry anthology - "A Hudson View" Poetry Digest - Winter 2008 International Collection. Visit with Ed Coet at "The Coet Blog" at http://thecoet.blogspot.com/.

www.ingramcontent.com/pod-product-compliance
Lightning Source LLC
Chambersburg PA
CBHW051843040426
42447CB00006B/670